HOCKEY CRAZY!

THIS IS A CARLTON BOOK
Published in 2018 by Carlton Books Limited,
an imprint of the Carlton Publishing Group,
20 Mortimer Street, London W1T 3JW

Text, design and illustration copyright
© Carlton Books Limited 2018

A catalogue record for this book is available
from the British Library.

ISBN: 978-1-78312-341-4

Printed in Dongguan, China
10 9 8 7 6 5 4 3 2 1

Executive Editor: Alexandra Koken
Design: RockJaw Creative
Senior Art Editor: Dani Lurie
Picture Research: Paul Langan
Production: Emma Smart

HOCKEY CRAZY!

SIMON MUGFORD

CONTENTS

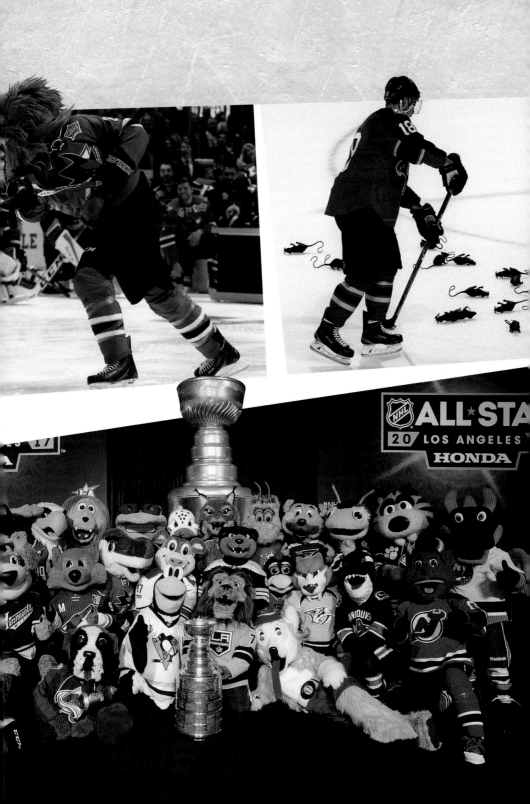

ICE-COOL LOOKS

Hockey fans are passionate about their sport and they are not shy about showing support for their team. When turning up in a team jersey isn't enough, there are plenty of hockey nuts ready to go the extra mile — or more — to show their devotion. Everything from animal outfits, fur coats and cat makeup, to a fan in a full-on astronaut suit has been spotted behind the boards. Some superfans of a particular player or coach even like to dress up as their hockey idol!

Going Green

There can be no hockey fans more dedicated to the art of dressing up than the Green Men. Since 2009, this pair of crazy Vancouver Canucks fans has attended games wearing bright-green spandex bodysuits. What better way to stand out from the crowd? Also known as Force and Sully, the duo sits next to the opposing team's penalty box and goofs around when a player is serving a penalty. Their outrageous antics include handstands, pretending to play golf and throwing frozen waffles in the air.

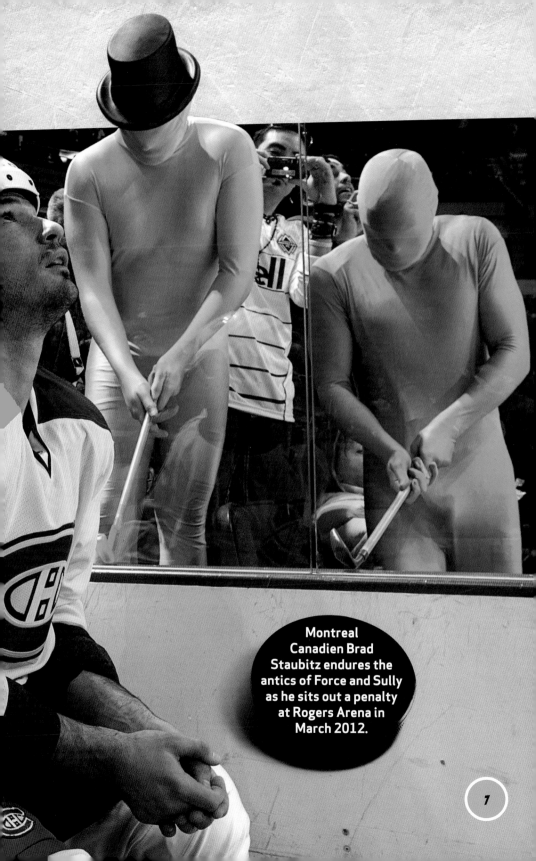

Montreal Canadien Brad Staubitz endures the antics of Force and Sully as he sits out a penalty at Rogers Arena in March 2012.

Hockey Mask Horror

The old-style goaltender masks may have been introduced to stop goalies getting injured, but they've gained an unexpected reputation all of their own. Jason, the bad guy in the 1980s horror film franchise Friday the 13th, wore a goaltender's mask and — bingo! Masks seemed scary, rather than just sensible. Nowadays, goalies go for a less frightening look.

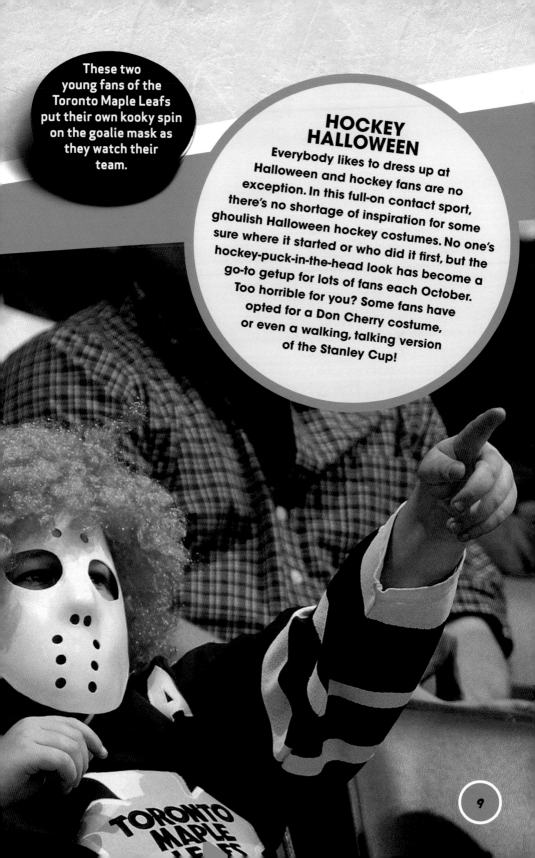

These two young fans of the Toronto Maple Leafs put their own kooky spin on the goalie mask as they watch their team.

HOCKEY HALLOWEEN

Everybody likes to dress up at Halloween and hockey fans are no exception. In this full-on contact sport, there's no shortage of inspiration for some ghoulish Halloween hockey costumes. No one's sure where it started or who did it first, but the hockey-puck-in-the-head look has become a go-to getup for lots of fans each October. Too horrible for you? Some fans have opted for a Don Cherry costume, or even a walking, talking version of the Stanley Cup!

CLASSIC CLASHES

You'll remember every game for something — a spectacular goal, a controversial call or a slick penalty shot. But some games stand out more than most. In a big international event like the Olympic Games, or a finals showdown between bitter rivals, the stakes are even higher. Throw a monster upset or a stupendous comeback into the mix and you have a classic hockey clash.

Team Canada celebrate their epic 1972 win in Moscow. Goal-scoring hero Paul Henderson is number 19 on the right.

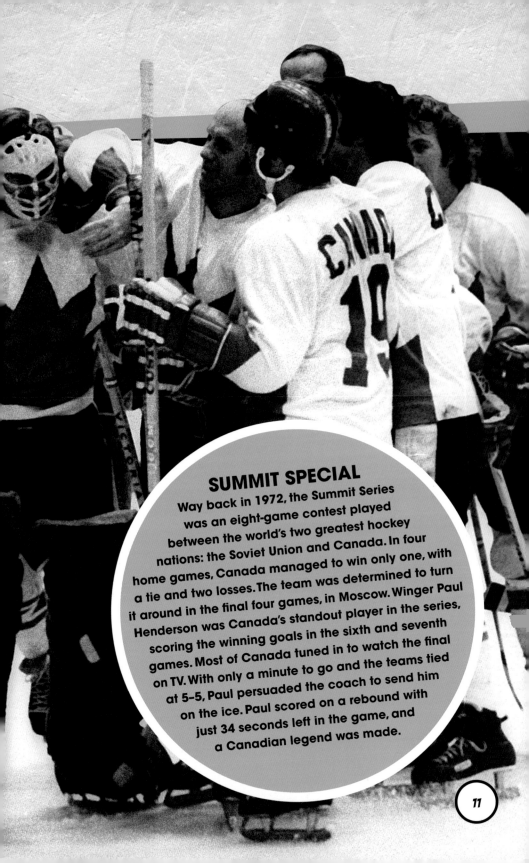

SUMMIT SPECIAL

Way back in 1972, the Summit Series was an eight-game contest played between the world's two greatest hockey nations: the Soviet Union and Canada. In four home games, Canada managed to win only one, with a tie and two losses. The team was determined to turn it around in the final four games, in Moscow. Winger Paul Henderson was Canada's standout player in the series, scoring the winning goals in the sixth and seventh games. Most of Canada tuned in to watch the final on TV. With only a minute to go and the teams tied at 5–5, Paul persuaded the coach to send him on the ice. Paul scored on a rebound with just 34 seconds left in the game, and a Canadian legend was made.

Nagano No-No

In 1998, the Winter Olympics in Nagano, Japan, welcomed professional National Hockey League (NHL) players for the first time — before that, the Games were for amateurs only. So you would expect the U.S. and Canadian teams to dominate, right? Well, that's not quite how it turned out. The Americans were dumped out of the quarter-finals by the Czech Republic, which then faced Canada in the semis. The game was tied, so it went to a shootout. Incredibly Team Canada did not use Wayne Gretzky in the shootout — which the Czechs won, leaving him in tears on the bench.

MIRACLE ON ICE

At the 1980 Winter Olympics in Lake Placid, U.S.A., the Soviet Union faced the U.S. to do battle for a medal. The Soviets were number one in the world and Olympic gold medallists since 1964, while the U.S. team were the underdogs — college players with an average age of 22. With 20 minutes to go, the Soviets led 3–2 but in an incredible two minutes, the U.S. scored twice and held on to win 4–3 in one of the biggest upsets in hockey history. It is known as the "Miracle on Ice."

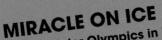

The U.S. players huddle in celebration after their incredible 1980 Olympic win over the Soviet Union.

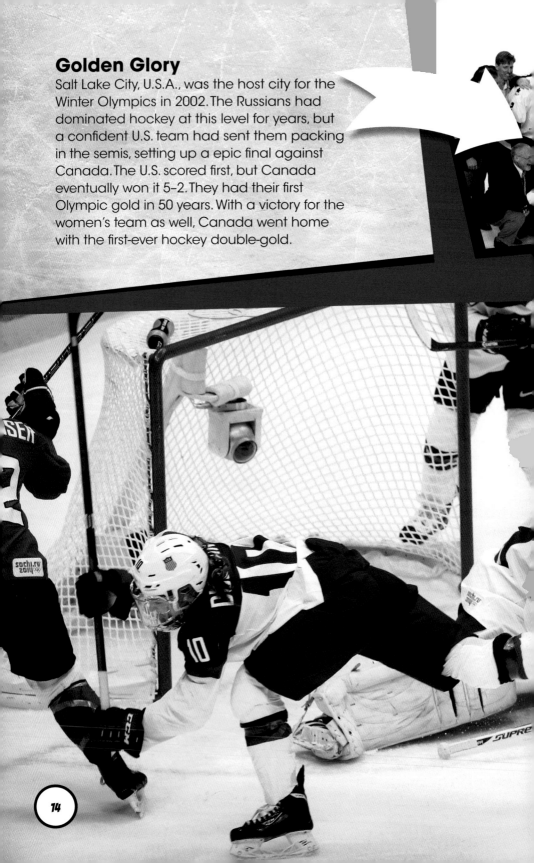

Golden Glory

Salt Lake City, U.S.A., was the host city for the Winter Olympics in 2002. The Russians had dominated hockey at this level for years, but a confident U.S. team had sent them packing in the semis, setting up a epic final against Canada. The U.S. scored first, but Canada eventually won it 5–2. They had their first Olympic gold in 50 years. With a victory for the women's team as well, Canada went home with the first-ever hockey double-gold.

SOCHI SUCCESS

The U.S. and Canadian women's hockey teams had been archrivals for two decades when they faced each other for the gold medal at the 2014 Winter Olympics in Sochi, Russia. The Americans were leading 2–1 with less than four minutes to go, but then Canada's Marie-Philip Poulin scored in the last minute to tie it up — and then won it in overtime.

Golden girl Marie-Philip Poulin (centre) celebrates her game-tying goal.

COOLEST GOALS

Great hockey goals tend to come in two flavours: ones that snatch an important victory from the jaws of defeat, or very impressive goals that look especially cool. Either way, a great goal can win a talented player a place in hockey history — or at least millions of views on YouTube.

Flying Bobby

The fourth and final game of the 1970 Stanley Cup Final between the Boston Bruins and the St. Louis Blues was tied at 3–3 when, 40 seconds into overtime, Boston defenceman Bobby Orr scored at the exact same time as he was tripped by Noel Picard of the Blues! The goal gave the Bruins their first Stanley Cup in 29 years, and Bobby's short flight was captured on camera to create one of the most famous photos in hockey.

Bobby Orr scored the fourth goal, in the fourth period of the game, while wearing the number 4 jersey and being tripped by player number 4.

Who Needs Two Hands?

Superstar Sidney Crosby has scored dozens of great goals in a dazzling career, including this incredible one-hander against the Buffalo Sabres in March 2017. The Pittsburgh Penguins' centre powered down the middle of the ice and flicked a single-handed backhander shot past the Sabres' goaltender Robin Lehner. Sidney had to use one hand because he was holding off a defenceman with the other! The strike was the 41st of the 44 that earned Sidney that season's Maurice Richard Trophy for leading goal-scorer.

SLIDING ALEX

Alex Ovechkin of the Washington Capitals had an awesome rookie season. One of its many highlights was a goal he scored against the Phoenix Coyotes in January 2006. It is frequently referred to as "one of the greatest goals of all time," and even "the Goal." Alex took the puck on a breakout and crossed inside the right circle, where he was brought down by Coyotes defenceman Paul Mara. Incredibly, while on his back and facing away from the goal, Alex managed to flick the puck into the net — to the astonishment of the players and crowd.

Sidney Crosby holds off the Sabres' Zach Bogosian with one hand while he scores with the other.

SUPER CELEBRATIONS

Sometimes a goal is just so good or important — or both — that it deserves a reaction that's a out of the ordinary. Then there are other times when a player just gets a bit overexcited and feels like showing off to his teammates and the fans, even if the goal wasn't that special. Of course there are people in the sport who frown on showboating, but a little spontaneous enthusiasm can be fun to watch!

Nail on His Knees

In 2013, Nail Yakupov was a young upstart playing for the Edmonton Oilers in his rookie season. In a game against the Los Angeles Kings, the Stanley Cup champions at the time, Nail scored a goal with just 4.7 seconds to go and forced the game into overtime. He marked the occasion by skating to centre ice and sliding all the way to the end of the rink — a sly reference to a celebration made famous by the Calgary Flames' Theo Fleury in their Stanley Cup victory over the Oilers in 1991. The young Russian had more to celebrate later as the Oilers went on to win the game 2-1.

Don Cherry said of Yakupov's slide: "If any time you want to make our highlights show, just act like an idiot like this."

Playoff Passions

It had been over 20 years since the New York Islanders last made it into the post-season. Finally in 2016 they were paired against the Florida Panthers in the first round. Going into game six, the Islanders were ahead in the series 3–2, but the Panthers started pushing back hard. The Panthers were leading the game 1–0 until the Islanders' John Tavares scored with only 54 seconds remaining. He followed that with a goal in overtime to claim the first series win for the New York team since 1993. Tavares — and many fans — were literally jumping for joy!

SWIMMING MILAN

Czech star Milan Hejduk played 14 seasons in the NHL, all with the Colorado Avalanche. In his record 1,020 games for them, Hejduk scored 375 goals. It's his reaction to netting the puck against the Dallas Stars in 2000 that's remembered the most though. His fantastic solo effort in overtime proved to be the winner, and the usually cool Hejduk immediately dove onto the ice and pretended to go for a swim in what has to be one of the silliest on-ice celebrations ever.

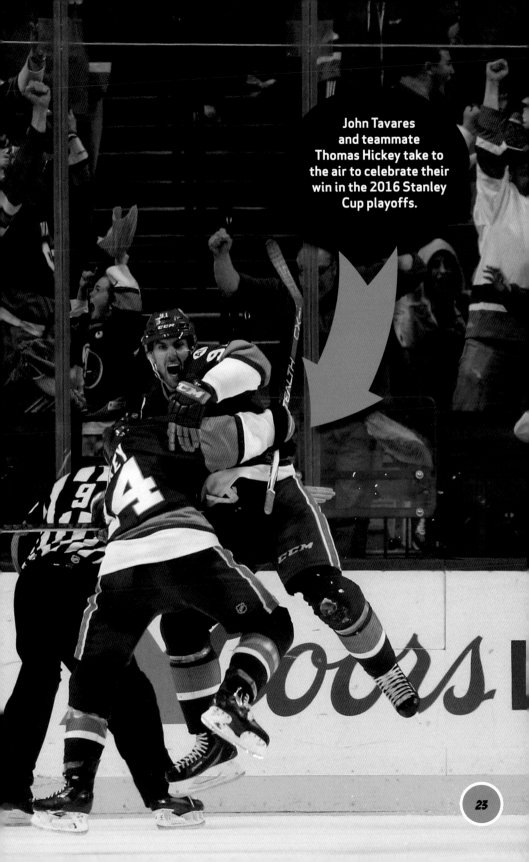

John Tavares and teammate Thomas Hickey take to the air to celebrate their win in the 2016 Stanley Cup playoffs.

THE STANLEY CUP

The most cherished prize in hockey, the Stanley Cup was first awarded over 120 years ago and is the oldest trophy in professional sports. Presented to the winner of the playoffs at the end of the NHL season, the Cup has a legendary, even mythical, status among hockey players. The name of everyone on the winning team is engraved on the trophy. When they run out of room, a new ring is added to the base, and the oldest ring is retired to the Hockey Hall of Fame.

PENGUIN POWER

The Pittsburgh Penguins won the Cup in 2017, beating the Nashville Predators to win the trophy for the second year in a row — the first team to do so since the Detroit Red Wings in 1997 and 1998. The game six win for the Penguins was not without controversy. An early Predators goal was ruled out with a blast from the referee's whistle, and then a puck that bounced into the side of the net scored the winning goal. But a win's a win, and the Penguins and Sidney Crosby went home with the Cup again.

It's a Cup. What Else Do You Do with It?

Plenty of players have taken a triumphant drink from Lord Stanley's bowl, but the famous silver Cup has also been filled with holy water to baptize children and used as a cereal bowl. The Kentucky Derby–winning racehorse Go for Gin ate from it in 1994, and Kris Draper of the Detroit Red Wings even let his toddler use it as a potty. Gross!

CUP ESCAPADES

Each player on the Cup-winning team gets to spend a day with the trophy. This tradition, started in 1995, has led to the Cup ending up in some unusual places. But even before 1995, crazy things happened to the Cup. Back in 1924, some Monteal Canadiens forgot it on the side of the road when they were fixing a flat tire and in 1940, when in the hands of the New York Rangers, it somehow managed to catch fire. When the Pittsburgh Penguins won it for the first time in 1991, the players decided to see if it would float in Mario Lemieux's swimming pool. It didn't. And Detroit Red Wings legend Steve Yzerman even took it into the shower with him!

The Montreal Canadiens have won the Stanley Cup 24 times — more than any other team!

AWESOME ARENAS

For hockey fans, the home-ice arena is a truly special place. It's where they go to see their heroes clash on the ice, where memories are made and friendships are formed. And then there are the venues built for special events like the Winter Olympics. These often showcase the very best in jaw-dropping stadium architecture.

BRILLIANT BOLSHOY

Built to host ice events at the 2014 Winter Olympics in Sochi, Russia, the Bolshoy Ice Dome is definitely one of the world's coolest-looking arenas. The venue hosted the historic "double-gold" wins for the Canadian men's and women's teams and is famous for its illuminated roof, which lights up the night sky with 38,000 colourful LED lights. This smart display features an animated puck whenever a goal is scored. Mysteriously, the cartoon puck failed to show up when the U.S. team scored against Russia, who lost to them 3–2.

SOCHI 2014

Big Bell

The Bell Centre is home to the most successful team in NHL history, the Montreal Canadiens. Together, the arena and the team capture the spirit of the game. With a capacity of 21,288, it's the NHL's largest arena. It has four wrap-around decks that give fans an awesome view from almost all parts of the stadium, plus state-of-the-art video and light shows. Taking in a game at the Bell Centre is a must for any die-hard fan.

HOCKEY'S CATHEDRAL

The Vaillant Arena in Davos, Switzerland, is one of the most impressive ice-skating venues in the world. Inside, an enormous arched wooden roof creates a fantastic atmosphere, and outside, the Vaillant boasts Europe's largest natural ice rink. Home to Davos Hockey Club, the arena is most famous for hosting the Spengler Cup, an annual international hockey tournament held between Christmas and New Year's.

THROW IT IN

So what do you do when your team scores a winning goal or makes it through to the playoffs? You throw stuff onto the ice, of course! Hockey fans have taken this tradition to heart over the years, and the range of stuff that gets lobbed over the glass just gets weirder and weirder . . .

Teddy-Bear Toss

Hockey fans sure are crazy, but they also have big hearts. The "teddy-bear toss" is a tradition for many hockey teams at Christmas. The fans throw stuffed animals onto the ice when the first goal is scored. After the game, the bears are collected and donated to children's charities. The Calgary Hitmen of the Western Hockey League (WHL) hold the record: 28,815 stuffed animals hit the ice in their game against the Swift Current Broncos in December 2015. It took 40 minutes to pick them all up!

The tradition of the teddy-bear toss was started by the Kamloops Blazers of the WHL, back in 1993.

More than 20 years after the original "rat trick," the Panthers still end up playing with plastic rats after a goal.

HAT TRICK

When a player scores a hat trick — three goals in one game — the fans celebrate by throwing their hats onto the ice. Hockey historians argue about where this tradition comes from, but one story has it that back in the 1930s, Toronto hat maker Sammy Taft offered a free hat to any player who scored three goals in a local NHL game. Fans can now mark this in their own way — just remember to write your name in your hat if you do!

Rat Trick

Back in 1995, Florida Panthers player Scott Mellanby was getting ready in the dressing room at Miami Arena when he saw a rat. Being a pro, Mellanby hit the rodent intruder with his stick and killed it! He scored two goals that night. After fans heard the rat story, they started throwing toy rats onto the ice whenever the Panthers scored. The NHL has tried to stop it and rival fans have even thrown rat traps in response!

MASCOT MADNESS

Since Harvey the Hound made his debut for the Calgary Flames in 1983, mascots have become a fixture at NHL games everywhere. These furry figures of fun can lift the spirits of the crowd when a team is losing, and get a bit overexcited when they're winning. Spot them dancing, falling over and even descending from the ceiling — it all adds to the fun!

#NHLAllSta

MASCOT SHOWDOWN

The NHL Mascot Showdown brings all the official mascots together once a year. They compete in a variety of events, including dodge ball, broomball, musical chairs and the finale — a mascot All-Star game. The competition is fierce but friendly, and above all, totally funny.

Al the Octopus is named after the Red Wings' building operations manager, Al Sobotka.

Octopus Al

The story of Al the Octopus starts in 1952 with Detroit Red Wings fans throwing dead octopuses (yes, you read that right) onto the ice. The octopuses' eight legs represented the eight playoff wins the Red Wings needed to win the Cup. Fans continued this bizarre tradition for years. Eventually, the team decided to create a less slimy mascot: a giant inflatable purple octopus. When the Red Wings reach the playoffs, Al gets raised above the ice to give the team an eight-legged boost.

Stuck Sharkie

S.J. Sharkie is the appropriately named mascot of
the San Jose Sharks. He's famous for an incident
back in 1999, when the Detroit Red Wings were in
town. Sharkie planned to impress the crowd by
lowering himself from the heights of the SAP Center
onto the ice. But poor Sharkie got stuck, suspended
12 metres (39 feet) above the ice, and the game
couldn't start with him dangling there. The TV
commentators were killing themselves laughing,
as has anyone who has seen the video
of poor Sharkie just hanging there.

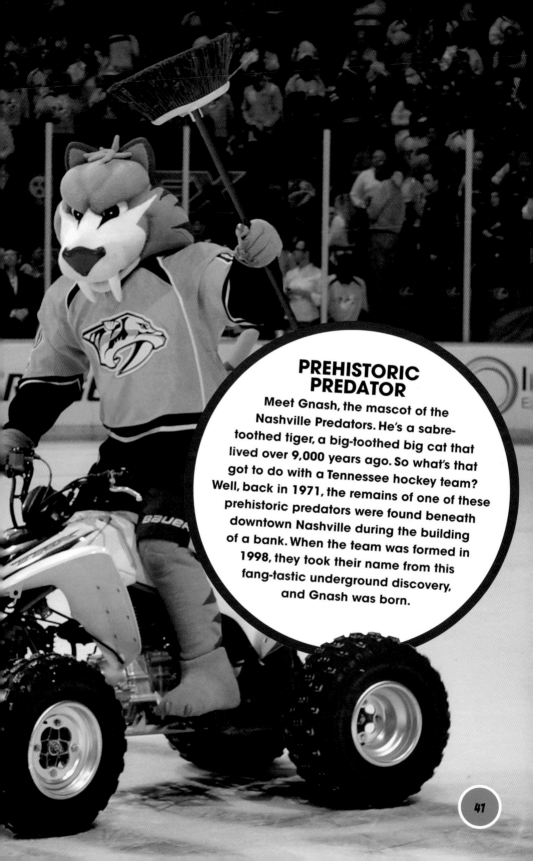

PREHISTORIC PREDATOR

Meet Gnash, the mascot of the Nashville Predators. He's a sabre-toothed tiger, a big-toothed big cat that lived over 9,000 years ago. So what's that got to do with a Tennessee hockey team? Well, back in 1971, the remains of one of these prehistoric predators were found beneath downtown Nashville during the building of a bank. When the team was formed in 1998, they took their name from this fang-tastic underground discovery, and Gnash was born.

RINK RITUALS

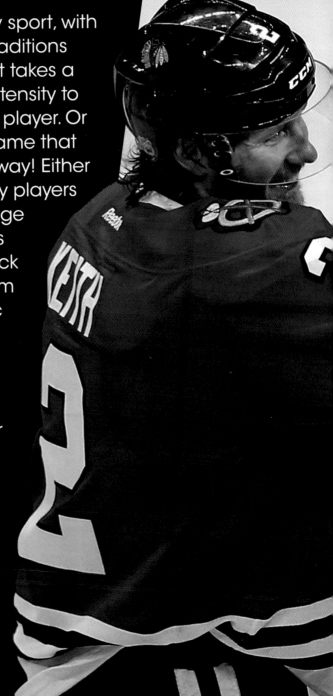

Hockey is a crazy sport, with its own unique traditions and rituals. And it takes a certain kind of intensity to be a pro hockey player. Or maybe it's the game that makes you that way! Either way, most hockey players have some strange and superstitious rituals to keep luck on their side. From eating a specific type of hot dog to wearing lucky underpants, you can be sure a hockey player or team has tried it for luck.

Brent Seabrook's rituals must have worked this time as he celebrates beating the Detroit Red Wings with Duncan Keith (left).

SERIOUS SEABROOK

Chicago Blackhawks defenceman Brent Seabrook is known as one of the most superstitious players in the NHL, if not in the whole of sport. As well as some unusual eating and sleeping routines, Brent always drives himself to the game, checks the clock in the team dressing room and then tapes his socks clockwise — always clockwise. Before going onto the ice, he repeats the same nine words over and over in his head, hugs his teammate Duncan Keith twice, and then eats seven chocolates.

Dung Good

Back in 1975, the New York Islanders made an incredible Stanley Cup comeback after losing the first three games against the Pittsburgh Penguins. What was their secret? When the Islanders had played at Madison Square Garden, the circus was also performing there and gave the team a bag of elephant poop as a gift. This unusual lucky charm travelled around with the Islanders for a year — and they kept on winning games!

A young Nashville Predators fan copies his heroes as they compete in the 2015 Stanley Cup playoffs.

THE PLAYOFF BEARD

The origins of the "playoff beard" tradition are shrouded in the mists of time. It is a superstition that means that players refuse to shave their beards during the entirety of the playoffs. Most people credit the New York Islanders with starting it during one of their four successful Stanley Cup runs in the early 1980s. It's essential not to shave once your team hits a winning streak during the playoffs. The craze has been adopted by other sports and plenty of fans like to get in on the act too.

ICE (RECORD) BREAKERS

Fans pack the Michigan Stadium in 2010 for the Big Chill at the Big House. And not one ice cream vendor in sight!

There are records still to be set in hockey but some may never be broken — due to rule changes, or because they were set by the unequalled Wayne Gretzky. The Philadelphia Flyers tied 24 games in the 1969–70 season, but since overtime was brought back and shootouts have been introduced to the regular season there are no more ties, so that record will stand forever! Then there is the 30-game winless streak that the luckless Winnipeg Jets endured in 1980–81 — no team wants to break that record!

BIG CHILL, BIG CROWD.

An outdoor college hockey game between the Michigan Wolverines and the Michigan State Spartans was attended by more people than any other hockey game in history. Some 113,411 fans braved near-freezing temperatures to watch the Wolverines win 5–0 at the Michigan Stadium. The game, which took place on December 11, 2010, is now known as the Big Chill at the Big House.

Mighty Mark

Are you ever too old to play hockey? Mark Sertich, a former hockey coach from Minnesota, was 95 years young (95 years and 4 days, to be exact) when he played in the Snoopy's Senior World Hockey Tournament in July 2016. Since retiring from coaching in 2012, Mark has continued to play hockey two or three times a week, usually with a team of local firefighters.

TRIPLE TOEWS

When Chicago Blackhawks captain Jonathan Toews won the Stanley Cup in 2010 at the age of 22, he became the youngest member of the Triple Gold Club. He had previously won the World Hockey Championships in 2007 and earned an Olympic gold at the 2010 Vancouver Games. Those three achievements meant Toews joined an elite club of some of the most decorated players in the game.

Super Per

Most hockey goals are fast, but some happen a bit more quickly than others. In a 1991 Danish First Division game, Per Olsen of Rungsted IK got himself a Guinness world record by scoring just two seconds after the game had started. The NHL record for superfast smashes into the net is five seconds after the start and is shared by three players: Doug Smail of the Winnipeg Jets (1981), Bryan Trottier of the New York Islanders (1984) and Alexander Mogilny of the Buffalo Sabres (1991).

Denis Kulyash celebrates his record-breaking supersmash with his KHL All-Star teammates.

KULYASH CLAPPER

The slapshot is the most powerful hockey shot of them all. The game's top players get the chance to show off their slapshots at All-Star skills events. At the 2012 event in Ottawa, Zdeno Chara of the Boston Bruins hit a 175.1 km/h (108.8 mph) effort. But that wasn't quite fast enough to break the world record, set in 2011 by Denis Kulyash of Avangard Omsk, who fired a 177.5 km/h (110.3 mph) slapper in the Russian Kontinental Hockey League's (KHL) version of the competition.

GOALIE GREATS

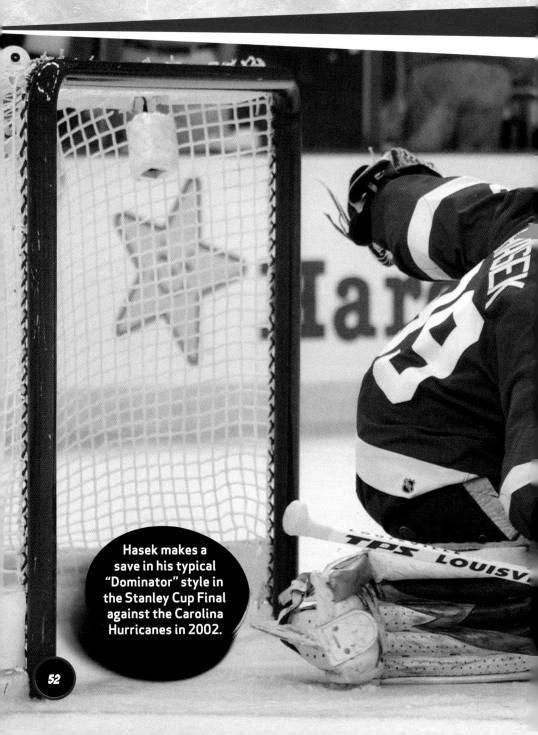

Hasek makes a save in his typical "Dominator" style in the Stanley Cup Final against the Carolina Hurricanes in 2002.

By now you know that it takes a special kind of crazy to be a hockey player. Well, for your average goaltender, you need to take that craziness and multiply it by 100 or more. It's one of the toughest positions to play in the game and, arguably, in any sport. Goalies tend to play the whole 60 minutes of the game, so they need plenty of endurance, plus the power and flexibility to switch between waiting around and leaping into action in a flash.

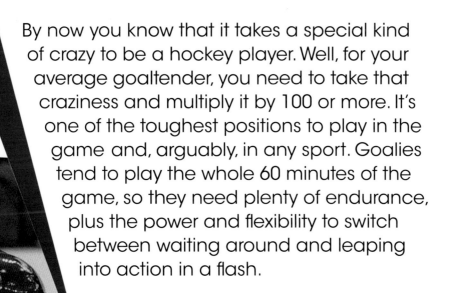

HYPER HASEK

Czech-born goalie Dominik Hasek played 16 seasons in the NHL between 1990 and 2008. He won the Stanley Cup twice with the Detroit Red Wings and won gold with the Czech Republic at the 1998 Olympics. He is regarded as one of the finest hockey goaltenders of all time, and in 2017, the NHL named Hasek to their list of the 100 Greatest NHL Players in history. Nicknamed the Dominator, he was incredibly flexible, able to twist his body and pull off the most unlikely saves from out of nowhere.

Finland's Finest

Finland, a country with only one-sixth the population of Canada, has provided the NHL with more than its fair share of goaltenders since the late 1990s. The country has focused on training goalies to move in front of the net in different ways, keeping their hands flexible. Urpo Ylonen is the legendary goaltending coach, still working in his seventies, who brought Finnish goalie greats such as Miikka Kiprusoff, Pekka Rinne and Niklas Backstrom to the NHL.

PLANTE THE PIONEER

Hockey was even crazier back in the 1950s! Goalies at the time didn't wear masks, but Jacques Plante, a goaltender for the legendary Montreal Canadiens team of the time, changed all that. Tired of having a face full of cuts, scars and stitches, and after a particularly bad broken nose, Jacques designed his own mask and started wearing it during games in 1959. By the mid-1960s, pretty much every goalie wore a mask. Jacques's goaltending was awesome. A Stanley Cup winner six times with the Canadiens, he was the first to come out of his crease regularly to play the puck. No one had played like that before! He was truly a pioneer of the modern game.

Marvellous Manon

Canadian goaltender Manon Rheaume broke new ground in 1992 by becoming the first woman to play in the NHL. She played in two exhibition games for the Tampa Bay Lightning, and went on to play in several minor professional leagues. Manon also won a silver medal with the Canadian women's team at the 1998 Winter Olympic Games.

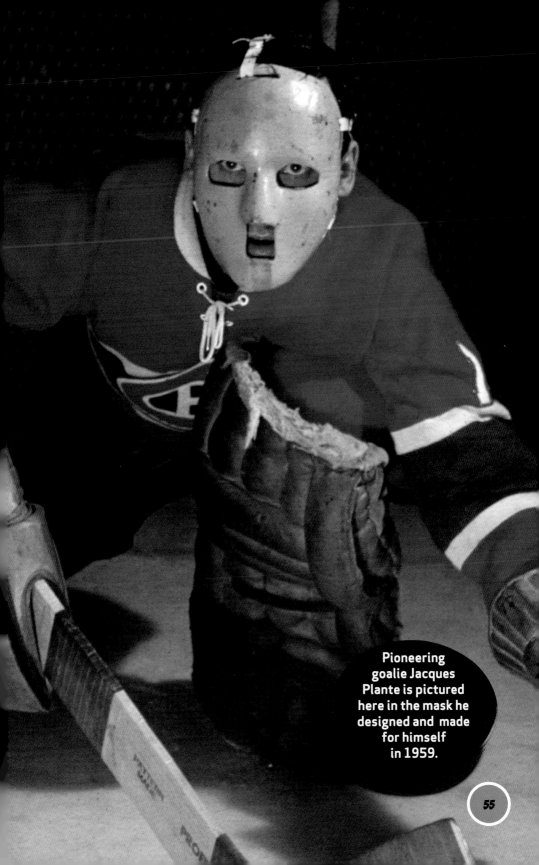

Pioneering goalie Jacques Plante is pictured here in the mask he designed and made for himself in 1959.

GOOFY GOALS

The empty net, the open goal. Often a blessing but sometimes a curse. A simple mistake by a goaltender or his defence can leave a goal wide open, making it easy for an opponent to tap the puck in and revel in the glory. But it doesn't always end that way. The player aims for the net but for some reason his mind goes blank, he fumbles the puck and misses — d'oh!

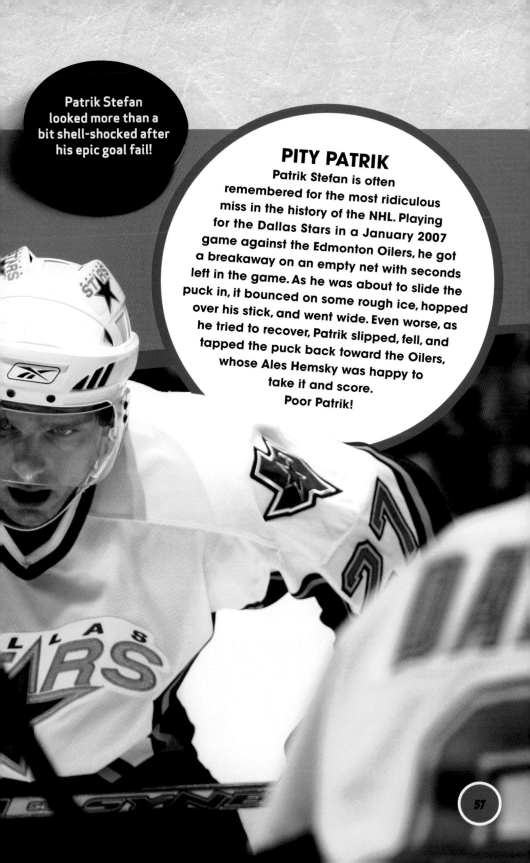

Patrik Stefan looked more than a bit shell-shocked after his epic goal fail!

PITY PATRIK

Patrik Stefan is often remembered for the most ridiculous miss in the history of the NHL. Playing for the Dallas Stars in a January 2007 game against the Edmonton Oilers, he got a breakaway on an empty net with seconds left in the game. As he was about to slide the puck in, it bounced on some rough ice, hopped over his stick, and went wide. Even worse, as he tried to recover, Patrik slipped, fell, and tapped the puck back toward the Oilers, whose Ales Hemsky was happy to take it and score.

Poor Patrik!

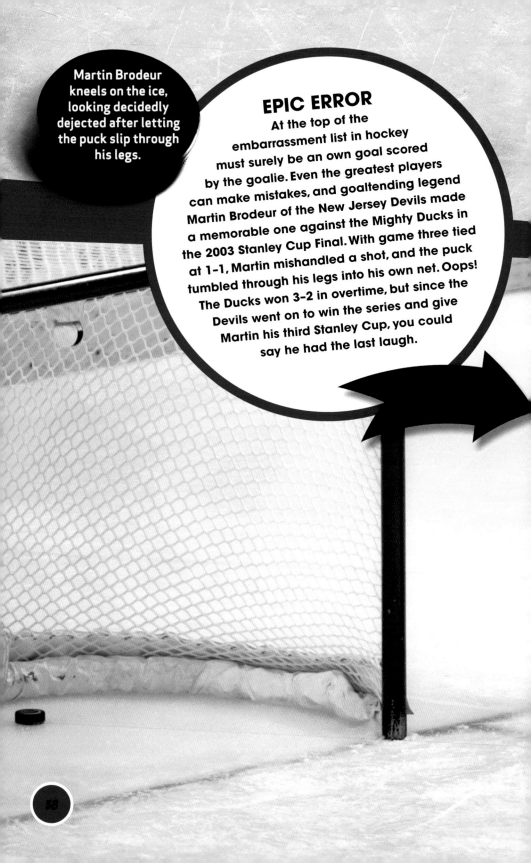

Martin Brodeur kneels on the ice, looking decidedly dejected after letting the puck slip through his legs.

EPIC ERROR

At the top of the embarrassment list in hockey must surely be an own goal scored by the goalie. Even the greatest players can make mistakes, and goaltending legend Martin Brodeur of the New Jersey Devils made a memorable one against the Mighty Ducks in the 2003 Stanley Cup Final. With game three tied at 1-1, Martin mishandled a shot, and the puck tumbled through his legs into his own net. Oops! The Ducks won 3-2 in overtime, but since the Devils went on to win the series and give Martin his third Stanley Cup, you could say he had the last laugh.

Whose Side Are You On?

Jeff Petry was playing for the Edmonton Oilers against the
Detroit Red Wings in a 2013 game when he attempted to
clear a rebound, only to hammer the puck into his own net.
The goal tied the game and sent it into overtime, which
the Red Wings went on to win. Jeff was born and raised in
Michigan, and he grew up in a family of Red Wings fans,
so maybe he just forgot which team he was playing for.

HOCKEY HILARITY

It can be tough spending a lot of time on the road, travelling from game to game in the company of the same group of teammates. Things can get kind of boring, so hockey players being . . . ya know, crazy and all, like to goof around to pass the time and keep each other entertained. From sticking fake snakes in the cooler to cutting a teammate's shoelaces and much, much worse, hockey has a long tradition of staging pranks and practical jokes.

Babies on the Bench

Hockey players like to come across as tough guys, but they're really softies inside! This rink poster has the hilarious side effect of making visiting players look like big babies on skates. Let's just hope none of them needs a diaper change!

The Erie Otters are a major junior team from Pennsylvania. Connor McDavid played for them from 2012–15.

Brent Burns and P.K. Subban (dressed as hockey legend Jaromir Jagr) yuk it up at the All-Star Skills Competition.

Skate Tape Trick

Generations of players have pulled this classic prank on one another. It's very simple; all that's needed is access to a player's skates in the dressing room when they're not looking. A small piece of clear tape placed along the middle of the skate blade will cause havoc the moment the player sets foot on the ice.

FUNNY GUYS

There are some players who take the art of pranking to a very high "skill" level. In the 1970s, Guy Lapointe was the Montreal Canadiens' self-appointed prankster king. He once shook hands with Prime Minister Pierre Trudeau with his hand covered in petroleum jelly. Today, the NHL's top funnyman is Brent Burns of the San Jose Sharks. Brent is serious about his hockey, but he loves having a laugh while going about it. The defenceman has such a long beard that he was once mistaken for a pirate on a visit to Disneyland, and he dressed as Chewbacca from Star Wars at the 2016 NHL All-Star Skills Competition Breakaway Challenge.

THE GREAT GRETZKY

Wayne Gretzky is quite simply the most famous hockey player in history. Known as the Great One, Gretzky played 20 seasons in the NHL, winning just about everything there is to win several times over. Not only is he the only player to score more than 200 points in a single season, but he did it four times. While playing for the Edmonton Oilers in the 1980s, he changed the way they played, making the team move together as a unit. Between 1982 and 1985, the Oilers became the highest-scoring team ever and won five Cups in seven years.

The Great One

Wayne was relatively small for a hockey player, but he made up for his build by being supersmart and creative. He could work out exactly where the puck would be at any given moment and respond. He could pass and shoot with a power and accuracy that left his opponents reeling. His influence on the modern game is immense.

After Wayne retired, the NHL retired his number, so no NHL player will wear the famous "99" again.

28

894

894 goals (the most ever)

19

Youngest player to score 50 goals in one season

215 215 points in one season (the most ever)

57

2,857 career points (the most ever)

200+ Three consecutive 200-plus point seasons

39 Games to score 50 goals

92 92 goals in a single season (the most ever)

SUPER SCORES

Records are always being set and broken in hockey. Rules change and players' skills improve, but some records from the early days still stand!

Super Mario

The Great One doesn't hold all of the hockey world records, just a lot of them. "Super" Mario Lemieux has a unique NHL record: he is the only player ever to score five goals five ways in one game. He scored a goal at even strength, one on a power play, another short-handed, another on a penalty shot and a final one into an empty net with one second left in the game. Stunning!

The high-scoring Slovakian women's team celebrate scoring against China at the 2010 Winter Olympics in Vancouver.

SUPER SCORE

In 2008, the women's teams of Slovakia and Bulgaria faced each other in a qualifying game for the 2010 Winter Olympics. After five minutes, Team Slovakia were leading 7–0, and by the end of the first period it was 31–0. The game ended 82–0, the highest-ever score in any IIHF-sanctioned event. The Slovakians qualified for the Vancouver Games, but were themselves soundly defeated 18-0 by Team Canada!

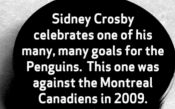

Sidney Crosby celebrates one of his many, many goals for the Penguins. This one was against the Montreal Canadiens in 2009.

HAB THAT!
You have to go all the way back to 1920 to find this record: most goals scored by a single team in an NHL game. The Montreal Canadiens were the dominant team of the time and they showed rivals the Quebec Bulldogs that they were the top dogs by beating them 16–3. Four players scored three or more times in a hammering that has not been matched since!

Sid the Kid

Since being drafted in 2005, the Pittsburgh Penguins' captain has achieved a huge amount at a young age. Among other records, Crosby is the youngest NHL player to score 100 points in a season, score 200 career points, make the starting lineup in an All-Star game, win the Art Ross Trophy, be the leading scorer in the playoffs and captain a Stanley Cup–winning team. Some kid!

Hayley takes a shot for Canada in the gold-medal game against the U.S.A. at the 2014 Winter Olympics.

Hayley Has It

Hayley Wickenheiser was the greatest female hockey player in the world. Growing up, Hayley often played on men's teams in the minor leagues. She went to Finland to play professional hockey, the first woman to play on a men's team in a position other than goalie. Not content with just her hockey accomplishments, Hayley has also played softball for Team Canada at the Summer Olympics!

Massive Medals

Hayley truly shone on the international hockey scene. Playing for Canada for 23 years, she has seven World Championship gold medals and six silvers. She represented Canada at five Olympic Winter Games, picking up four gold medals and one silver. She is the all-time Olympic points leader — men and women — with 51 (18 goals, 33 assists). Hayley retired from her playing career in 2017.

4
Olympic gold medals

7
World Championship gold medals

1
Olympic silver medal

6
World Championship silver medals

18
Olympic goals scored

276
International appearances

168
International goals

ZIPPY ZAMBONIS

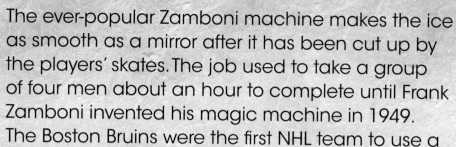

The ever-popular Zamboni machine makes the ice as smooth as a mirror after it has been cut up by the players' skates. The job used to take a group of four men about an hour to complete until Frank Zamboni invented his magic machine in 1949. The Boston Bruins were the first NHL team to use a Zamboni, in 1954. Watching the Zamboni drive around the rink during the break has been the highlight of the game experience ever since.

SHARKS ON ICE

Ice resurfacers are often customized by the team to add a bit more fun. The San Jose Sharks have one of the best-known Zambonis. With a dorsal fin and menacing shark-tooth smile, it's quite a sight as it eats up the ice. A few lucky fans have even had the chance to hitch a ride on it!

Cult of Cute

The Zamboni machine has a hypnotic effect on hockey fans — there's just something about the way it slowly moves over the ice, smoothing it out to glossy perfection. You can't help but watch. The hypnotic powers of ice resurfacers make them perfect for advertising and promotional events at games — all eyes are on the Zamboni!

This special Zamboni promoting marshmallow Peeps for Easter even has a friend to keep it company out on the ice.

SMOOTH MOVES

Everyone knows the Zamboni machine goes very slowly, but it travels a long way! On average, the Zamboni machine covers over 6 kilometres (4 miles) in every game. Over one year, all that ice resurfacing fun adds up to more than 3,000 km (2,000 miles)! In the run-up to the 2002 Winter Olympics, a Zamboni machine was driven coast to coast across Canada — a kind of slow-motion version of an Olympic torch relay. The 5,954 km (3,700 mile) trip took nearly nine months to complete!

4625

C

Peeps

BU

HOCKEY TOUGH GUYS

Hockey's a demanding game, so the people who play it tend to be tough! And none are meaner than the players known as the enforcers. They get in and defend their team's star player when he's getting a bit too much attention from their opponents. They put themselves in the way of an attack or a shot and start to get physical when the going gets tough. Of course, the best enforcers impress with their playing ability too!

Big Georges

At 1.93 m and 111 kg (6'4" and 245 lbs.), enforcers do not come much bigger than former Oilers, Penguins and Canadiens player Georges Laraque. Throughout his 11-season NHL career, Big Georges could definitely make his presence known on the ice. He's a big, tough guy for sure, but at heart he's a gentleman and a bit of a softie. Since retiring in 2010, Georges, an animal-loving vegan, was deputy leader of the Green Party of Canada until 2013, and has invested in a vegan restaurant and a health company.

Georges would smash himself against the glass when the Oilers scored. This was known as the "Laraque Leap."

FADING FIGHTS

Hockey is quite a bit different now than it was in Gordie's day. In the last 20 years or so, the fans' appetite for fights on the ice has been replaced with an enthusiasm for watching their heroes, well, play hockey! Fighting is banned at the Olympic level, and though it still happens sometimes in the NHL, the days of entire teams brawling on the ice are, thankfully, over . . . mostly.

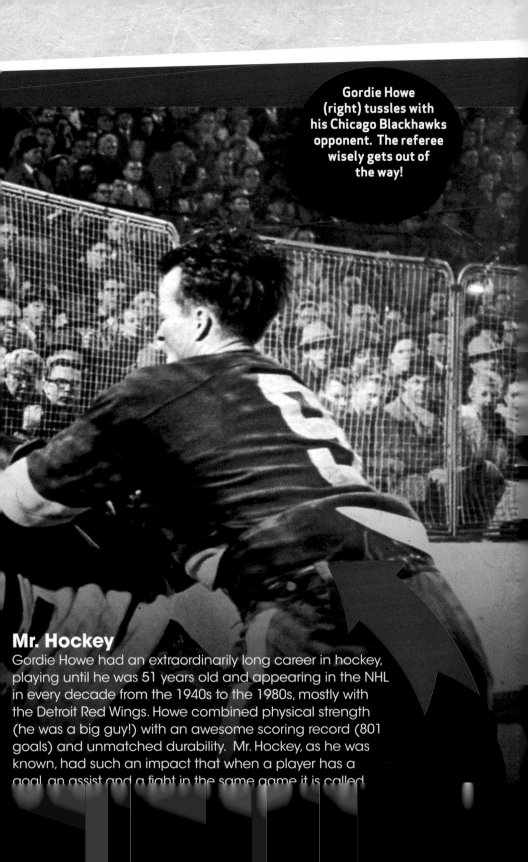

Gordie Howe (right) tussles with his Chicago Blackhawks opponent. The referee wisely gets out of the way!

Mr. Hockey

Gordie Howe had an extraordinarily long career in hockey, playing until he was 51 years old and appearing in the NHL in every decade from the 1940s to the 1980s, mostly with the Detroit Red Wings. Howe combined physical strength (he was a big guy!) with an awesome scoring record (801 goals) and unmatched durability. Mr. Hockey, as he was known, had such an impact that when a player has a goal, an assist and a fight in the same game it is called

KEEP IT IN THE FAMILY

Brothers have played against each other on rival teams five times in the Stanley Cup playoffs.

There is a long and fine tradition of hockey-focused families. Since the NHL was founded in 1917, 26 players have played for the same team that their fathers did, and no fewer than 47 pairs of brothers have taken to the ice together as teammates. The great Gordie Howe went one further and actually played with his sons Mark and Marty for one season with the Hartford Whalers.

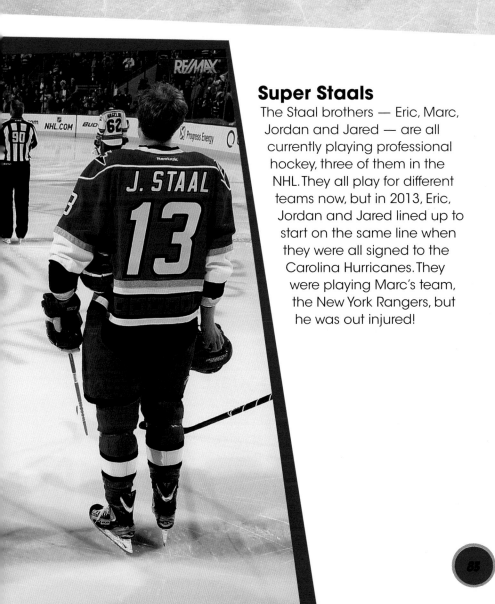

Super Staals

The Staal brothers — Eric, Marc, Jordan and Jared — are all currently playing professional hockey, three of them in the NHL. They all play for different teams now, but in 2013, Eric, Jordan and Jared lined up to start on the same line when they were all signed to the Carolina Hurricanes. They were playing Marc's team, the New York Rangers, but he was out injured!

Oh, Brother!

The Sutter family is something of a legend when it comes to producing hockey players. No fewer than six brothers have played in the NHL. Gary, the seventh brother, chose to stick to farming instead, but his brothers say he's the best player of them all! Naturally, there is now a second generation of hockey-playing Sutters and three of them have already played in NHL.

SEEING DOUBLE

Henrik and Daniel Sedin share many things. A mom and dad, for one. Also, birthdays and looks. Yes, these brothers from Sweden are identical twins and they also shared a hockey team — the Vancouver Canucks. They were both drafted by the Canucks in 1999 and spent their entire 17-season careers there. Henrik was the captain, while Daniel was the alternate captain and the Canucks' all-time top goal scorer.

The Sedin twins. Henrik is on the left; Daniel is on the right. Or is it the other way around?

ICE ODDITIES

There are some hockey stories that are just too weird to categorize. Did you know that the Anaheim Ducks are named after the fictional team in the Disney movie *The Mighty Ducks*? Or that before the 1927–28 season, players were not allowed to pass the puck forward? And before the 2017–18 season, wannabe goalies had a chance to take to the ice. NHL rules said that if a team's goalies were both injured, then anyone could be picked to play — even a fan from the stands!

Giant Player

The world's largest hockey stick is displayed outside the Cowichan Arena in Duncan, British Columbia. It has to be outside — it's over 61 m (200 feet) long and weighs more than 27,000 kg (60,000 lbs.)! And there is a puck too. It certainly attracts plenty of interest from tourists, but to date, no giant-sized players have turned up wanting to play with it!

The world's largest hockey stick and puck are 40 times life size.

Flying Fathers

The Flying Fathers were a group of hockey-playing priests who played exhibition games to raise money for charity. Founded in 1963 by Les Costello and Brian McKee, they toured all over North America, raising more than $4 million for good causes.

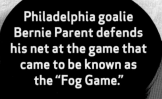
Philadelphia goalie Bernie Parent defends his net at the game that came to be known as the "Fog Game."

THE FOG AND THE BAT

Probably one of the strangest games in a Stanley Cup Final took place in May 1975. The Buffalo Sabres and the Philadelphia Flyers were playing game three at the Buffalo Memorial Auditorium when a mist formed over the ice. A combination of hot, humid weather and no air conditioning created the fog, and the players and fans could barely see. The game was stopped five times while players and rink workers skated around waving towels to try to waft the fog away. And then a bat swooped down from the arena roof, adding to the surreal atmosphere. Despite all the spooky goings-on, the Sabres eventually won, 5–4.

GEAR TALK

Hockey is a straightforward game, but you do need some basic equipment to play. Skates, a stick and a puck will get you started, plus protective gear that will stop you from getting hurt. Hockey gear has come a long way since the early days. Hundreds of years ago — or longer! — hockey-like games were played out on frozen lakes, with apples, slices of tree stumps or even chunks of frozen cow dung used as pucks.

As the game moved indoors, pucks made from sliced-up lacrosse balls began to be used. Rubber pucks showed up in the early 1900s. At first, they were made by gluing pieces of rubber tires together, but those were soon replaced by the solid rubber versions in use today.

GET PUCKY

The standard puck used in most professional hockey leagues is a 2.5 cm (1 inch) thick, 7.6 cm (3 inch) in diameter solid rubber disc. Pucks often have a team or sponsor's logo printed on one or both sides. Pucks are usually kept in a freezer, as a frozen puck will glide smoothly across the ice and is less likely to bounce.

Sick Sticks

Back in the 1800s, hockey sticks were made by hand from a single piece of wood. Later, the blades were made separately and inserted into the shaft of the stick. Until the 1960s, all sticks had straight blades, but then Chicago Blackhawks forwards Stan Mikita and Bobby Hull noticed that they could fire the puck better with a broken (and therefore, slightly curved) blade. From then on, the use of curved stick blades became the norm and changed hockey shooting and passing forever.

Mr. Hockey himself, Gordie Howe, checks out Stan and Bobby's crazy curved blades that would go on to change the game.

HEADS FIRST

In the crazy old days of hockey there was no rule about wearing a helmet, so hardly any players did. After a number of serious injuries in the 1960s and 1970s, more players started to wear them. In 1979 the NHL ruled that all new players had to wear helmets but that those who had signed before 1979 did not, so a few old hands played on without them. Craig MacTavish, who played his final game for the St. Louis Blues in 1997, was the last NHL player to play without a helmet.

FREAK SHOTS AND GOALS

Sometimes in this game, goals seem to come out of nowhere. The puck is moving so fast that it disappears from sight and then turns up in a place that nobody expects. All it takes is a little bump on the ice or a crowded goal crease and any number of crazy things can happen.

The Olympic Netbuster

The Canadiens' Shea Weber has one of the hardest slapshots in the game, and regularly hits the puck at near-record speeds of over 174 km/h (108 mph). When playing for Canada against Germany in the 2010 Winter Olympics, one of Weber's shots was so hard that it burst straight through the net and out the other side! Everyone watching assumed it was a miss (after all, the puck didn't stay in the net), but the instant replay showed it was a goal.

Occasionally even protective Plexiglas needs to be replaced, like in this Winter Olympics game in 2010!

Mark Pysyk of the Sabres celebrates at the expense of poor Mike Smith, who has just dropped the puck out of his pants!

Trouser Trick

Arizona Coyotes goalie Mike Smith had a wardrobe malfunction in a game against the Buffalo Sabres in 2013. During overtime, the puck was hit into the air near the goal . . . and then disappeared. Confused players skated around searching for it and TV commentators wondered where the puck had gone. And where was it? In Smith's pants — and to make matters worse, Smith then unwittingly plopped the puck into his own goal. Oops.

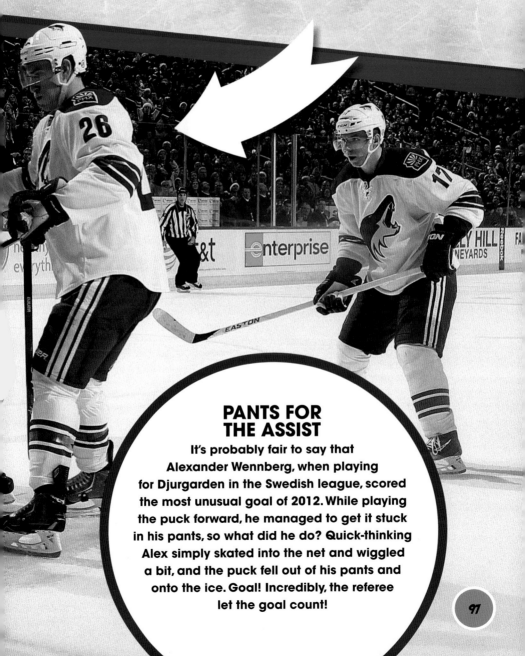

PANTS FOR THE ASSIST

It's probably fair to say that Alexander Wennberg, when playing for Djurgarden in the Swedish league, scored the most unusual goal of 2012. While playing the puck forward, he managed to get it stuck in his pants, so what did he do? Quick-thinking Alex simply skated into the net and wiggled a bit, and the puck fell out of his pants and onto the ice. Goal! Incredibly, the referee let the goal count!

STARS ON ICE

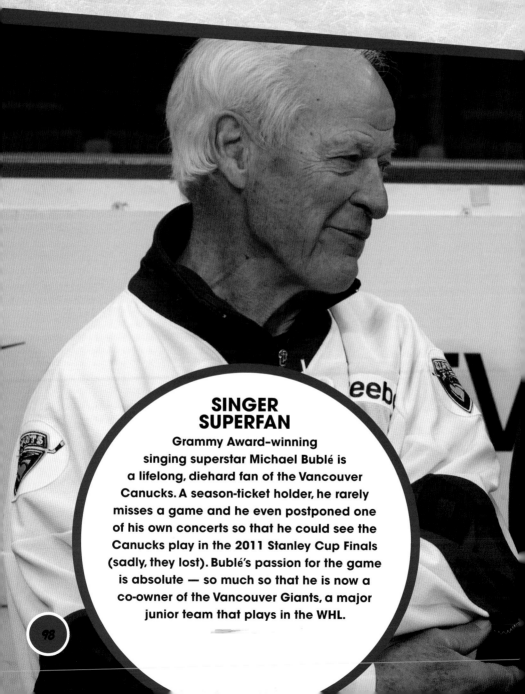

SINGER SUPERFAN

Grammy Award-winning singing superstar Michael Bublé is a lifelong, diehard fan of the Vancouver Canucks. A season-ticket holder, he rarely misses a game and he even postponed one of his own concerts so that he could see the Canucks play in the 2011 Stanley Cup Finals (sadly, they lost). Bublé's passion for the game is absolute — so much so that he is now a co-owner of the Vancouver Giants, a major junior team that plays in the WHL.

Everyone loves hockey, don't they? Of course they do, and that includes the rich and the famous. There are plenty of movie stars, music makers, stars of other sports and celebrity YouTubers who love some rinkside action. Anyone who is anyone just can't get enough of hockey.

Michael Bublé, pictured here with the late, great Gordie Howe, with whom he co-owned the Vancouver Giants.

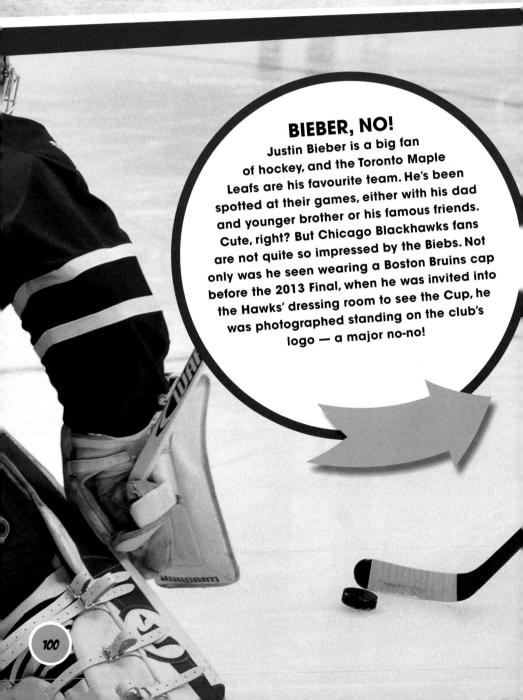

Hockey-Crazy Carell

Hollywood funny-man Steve Carell (the voice of Gru in the Despicable Me movies) is a lifelong Boston Bruins fan. He was a goalie growing up and still plays today in a league in Los Angeles. He even has his own entry on Elite Prospects, an online database of hockey players.

BIEBER, NO!

Justin Bieber is a big fan of hockey, and the Toronto Maple Leafs are his favourite team. He's been spotted at their games, either with his dad and younger brother or his famous friends. Cute, right? But Chicago Blackhawks fans are not quite so impressed by the Biebs. Not only was he seen wearing a Boston Bruins cap before the 2013 Final, when he was invited into the Hawks' dressing room to see the Cup, he was photographed standing on the club's logo — a major no-no!

Toronto Maple Leafs fan Justin Bieber took to the ice for some holiday fun in December 2011.

HOCKEY KIDS

Young hockey fans are always a welcome sight at games. Whether they're getting a massive furry hug from a supersize mascot, cheering on their heroes with everything they've got or being wowed by the sheer size of the stadium and the dazzling screens, the sight of kids enjoying a game is guaranteed to melt the hardest of hockey fan hearts.

Tyler Terror

Two-year-old Tyler Avolia's reaction to seeing his team score has been watched by people all over the world. When the Pittsburgh Penguins scored in a Stanley Cup playoff game in 2014, Tyler's fierce goal celebration was seen on television, then shared on YouTube and quickly went viral. With his fists pumping and his face screwed up, little Tyler's intense game face made him a massive hit with hockey fans that year.

This young fan is enjoying the action at the rink! Just as long as those teeth aren't too sharp...

Tomorrow's Superstars

You're never too young to start playing hockey!
Canadian kids can take part in hockey leagues
and recreational programs. One of these programs
is the Timbits Minor Sports Program, where kids
focus on learning, friends and fun. Sometimes
Timbits teams even get to go out on the ice
during breaks at NHL games.

TOP STARS

Two of today's hottest young hockey players, Connor McDavid and Auston Matthews, both started out in minor league hockey when they were really, really young! The NHL's top rookie of 2017, Auston started playing at age five, with the Arizona Bobcats. Connor, the 2017 winner of the Ted Lindsay Award and the Art Ross and Hart Memorial Trophies, started minor hockey at the age of four!

Timbits teams playing between periods at the Calgary Saddledome in 2016.

ONE-ON-ONE FUN

NHL veteran Bob Essensa stops superstar Mark Messier on a penalty shot in the 2016 Heritage Classic Alumni game.

The one-on-one is one of the most tense moments of play in hockey. It's a shooter-versus-goalie, eyeball-to-eyeball, do-or-die situation. Whether it's a penalty shot, a shootout or an exciting breakaway, shooters will try every slick trick and serious skill they know — and maybe make up some new ones! — in order to score in this battle of nerve, talent and steel.

Pure Ballet

During a KHL skills competition. Russian forward Nikita Gusev performed a stunning between-the-legs trick goal. After lifting the puck off the ice, Nikita did a 360° spin like a ballet dancer and finished with a flying shot that whipped past goalie Stanislav Galimov. It probably wouldn't happen in an actual game, but it was still an amazing goal.

Magic Move

Awesome trickery is on display at every level of the sport. Nicklas Lindberg was playing for the Port Huron Icehawks against the Kalamazoo Wings in the ECHL (East Coast Hockey League) when he fooled goalie Joel Martin in a shootout by switching his stick from right to left — behind his back! — and hammering the puck into the goal. Super slick!

The Tampa Bay Lightning's Dan Ellis can only look on as Linus Omark's sublime shot slides past him and into the net.

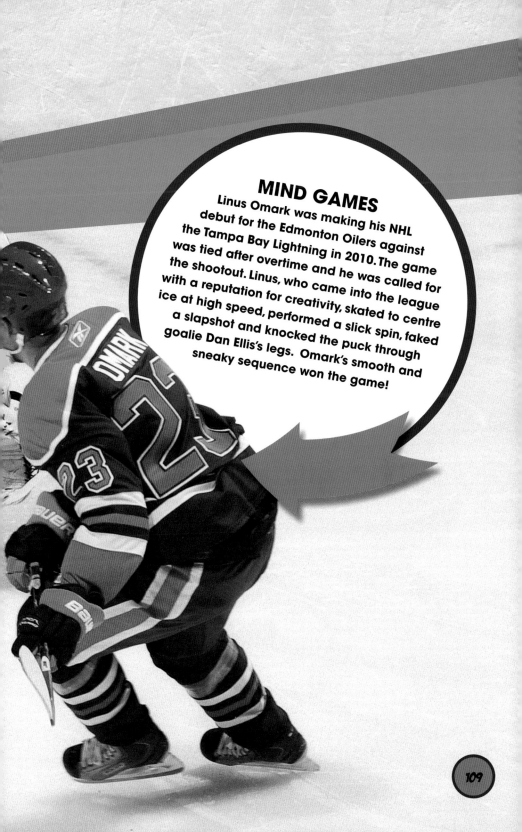

MIND GAMES

Linus Omark was making his NHL debut for the Edmonton Oilers against the Tampa Bay Lightning in 2010. The game was tied after overtime and he was called for the shootout. Linus, who came into the league with a reputation for creativity, skated to centre ice at high speed, performed a slick spin, faked a slapshot and knocked the puck through goalie Dan Ellis's legs. Omark's smooth and sneaky sequence won the game!

In It Goes!

Young Edmonton Oilers captain Connor McDavid scored on a supersweet penalty shot against the team's archrivals, the Calgary Flames, in 2016. In the first game at Edmonton's new Rogers Place arena, Connor used almost every move in the book, flicking the puck from side to side at high speed before slotting it past the poor Flames goalie Brian Elliott at close range.

Toronto Maple Leaf Mikhail Grabovski squares up for another shot against the St. Louis Blues. This one, however, is spinarama free.

SPINARAMA

For many years, a favourite move for penalty shots and shootouts was the spinarama. There are many flashy examples of players speeding toward the goal, then stopping and turning a full 360° before shooting. Mikhail Grabovski of the Maple Leafs perfected the spinarama and hit it home in front of a helpless St. Louis Blues goalie in 2011. Amazing as that sounds, you're unlikely to see this move now because the NHL banned it in 2014.

RINK RIVALS

Hockey players — and their fans — are competitive and fiercely loyal to their teams, which can lead to heated rivalries between clubs. In the earliest days of the NHL, for instance, all the teams were based in Central Canada. They played frequently and had a long history of playoff wins, losses and grudges. To this day, the Montreal Canadiens and the Toronto Maple Leafs remain fierce rivals! It's just a fact of life that when two rival teams meet on the ice, the atmosphere will be electric — and the grudges can last for decades.

Battle of Alberta

The intense rivalry between the Edmonton Oilers and the Calgary Flames dates back to 1980, when the Flames moved from Atlanta to Calgary, bringing the teams closer together. The Oilers were at their Gretzky-led peak, but the Flames had stars of their own. Both teams dominated the league, with one or the other making every Stanley Cup Final from 1983 to 1990. The Oilers won five Stanley Cups and the Flames just one. Recent years have not seen the same level of success for either team, but for the fans and players, the "Battle of Alberta" remains one of the most hotly contested games in hockey.

The Battle of Alberta is as intensely fought as ever. In this 2016 encounter, there is plenty of pushing and shoving in the crease.

Canadiens versus Maple Leafs

The rivalry between the Montreal Canadiens and the Toronto Maple Leafs is the oldest in the NHL. Both teams have huge followings. From 1938 to 1970, they were the only Canadian teams in the league, so fans across the country picked one or the other to support. The rivalry also reflects the competition between cities — French-speaking Montreal and English-speaking Toronto. For decades these two teams dominated the NHL. The Canadiens have won 24 Stanley Cups to the Maple Leafs' 11, but neither team has won the Cup since the 1990s.

FRIENDS AND NEIGHBOURS?

The rivalry between the U.S. and Canadian women's teams is as intense as anything in the NHL, probably even more so. In the NHL, the teams at least get to let off steam against their rivals in regular encounters, but the women's national teams only meet at big tournaments and the Olympics — allowing plenty of time for tensions to simmer. They have faced each other in every Olympic and World Championship final since they began. Canada dominates the Olympic record with four golds, but the U.S. has won gold twice. In World Championship action, Canada just edges their rivals in wins. When Canada and the U.S. face off, it's always a thrilling encounter!

Team USA's Monique Lamoureux and Jenny Potter battle Canada's Rebecca Johnston for the puck in the 2010 Olympic hockey final.

KING COACHES

A good coach can make the difference between a good team and an excellent team. The coach is central to how the whole team — on-ice players and rinkside staff — work together. To lead, encourage younger talent, and keep the big stars and personalities in line, it can help to be a big character. But at the end of the day, what really counts as a coach is winning, and Scotty Bowman was the best at that, winning 1,244 regular-season games and 9 Stanley Cups in a 30-season career.

Planet of the Grapes

Don Cherry is famous today for being a hockey commentator. Well known for his outrageous suits and outspoken opinions, at one time he was also a coach. He won 250 regular-season games and 31 playoff games as coach of the Boston Bruins and the Colorado Rockies. He took the Bruins to the Stanley Cup Final twice, but never managed to win it.

You can always spot Don Cherry in a crowd! Here he is, in typical understated style, reporting on the 2009 Stanley Cup Final.

Cooper's Quips

Tampa Bay Lightning coach Jon Cooper has become well known for his funny quotes in press conferences and post-game interviews. After losing 5–0 to the Boston Bruins, he said, "The only thing good about tonight was the national anthem." And after snatching a win over the Buffalo Sabres: "I was looking for the police when we left the locker room because I thought we'd get arrested for stealing. We stole two points."

COACH ACE

The most successful coach working in the NHL today, Joel Quenneville began coaching in the NHL with the St. Louis Blues in 1996 and took them to the playoffs every year that he was coach. After a few seasons with the Colorado Avalanche, Quenneville took over the helm of the Blackhawks in 2008. They have made the playoffs in every season since and won the Stanley Cup three times. After winning his 783rd game in 2016, he became the NHL's second-most successful coach ever, after Scotty Bowman.

OFFICIAL OFF-DAYS

When hockey referees get it wrong and flub a call, boy do they get a hard time from the crowd! There are few things worse for fans and players than losing because of a blown call. Technology can help keep things fair with instant replay cameras watching from all angles, but referees are still at the heart of the action on the ice. As a fan, you've just got to hope that the referee doesn't have an off-day while your team is playing.

Gretzky's High Stick

One of the most famous blown calls in hockey explains why Toronto Maple Leafs fans have little time for Wayne Gretzky. It was 1993 and the Maple Leafs were tied 4–4 in overtime with Gretzky's Los Angeles Kings in game six of the Stanley Cup Conference Finals. If the Leafs won, they would make their first Final for 25 years. Gretzky took a shot and lifted his stick high, cutting Doug Gilmour's chin open. It should have been a penalty, but referee Kerry Fraser didn't see it. No penalty, no Stanley Cup Final for the Leafs. It has been many, many years since it happened and some Leafs fans are still not over it.

Any Maple Leafs fans should look away now — here's Gretzky celebrating the hat trick he scored in the infamous game.

Referee Rumble

Referees and officials often get a taste of the fast and furious on-ice action. They might make contact with a raised stick, find themselves in the flight path of a rogue puck or have to put themselves between two players that are having a "disagreement." All refs are swift and skilful on their skates, but the occasional collision, where the one in stripes finds himself flat out on the ice, is inevitable.

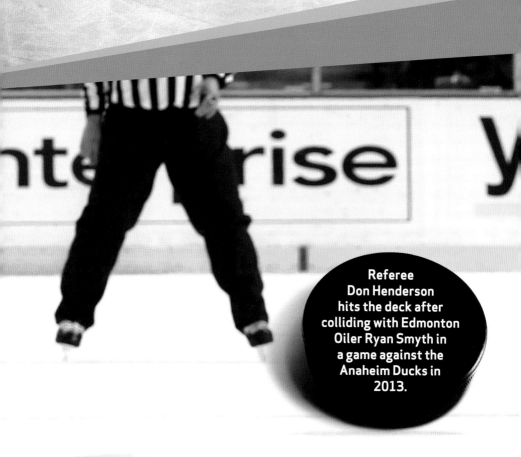

Referee Don Henderson hits the deck after colliding with Edmonton Oiler Ryan Smyth in a game against the Anaheim Ducks in 2013.

HOME ICE ADVANTAGE?

When the Winter Olympics came to Salt Lake City in 2002, the American women were confident of beating their northern rivals. Having won the first-ever women's Olympic hockey final four years earlier, they felt that playing at home meant they had another gold in the bag. When, to the surprise of many, American referee Stacey Livingston was appointed to run the game, the Canadians cried foul. And when Livingston awarded no less than 13 penalties against Canada, it started to feel like a set-up. But, against these odds, Canada held off the U.S. in the power plays and won 3–2 to claim their very first Olympic gold.

PLAYER NICKNAMES

So long as there are people playing hockey, players will give each other nicknames. Here are some of the best:

GEORGES VEZINA, "THE CHICOUTIMI CUCUMBER,"
because the goalie was cool as a cucumber in the net.

BERNIE "BOOM BOOM" GEOFFRION,
because he had a fantastic slapshot.

BOBBY HULL, "THE GOLDEN JET,"
because he was blond and fast.

WAYNE GRETZKY, "THE GREAT ONE."
No explanation required.

GORDIE HOWE, "MR. HOCKEY,"
because he loved the game and it loved him.

"TERRIBLE" TED LINDSAY,
because he was small and mean.

DON "GRAPES" CHERRY,
because it's all about the fruit.

HAYLEY "CHICKEN" WICKENHEISER
because . . . "Chickenheiser."

HILARY "THE EVENING" KNIGHT,
because the evening is before the night!

MAURICE "ROCKET" RICHARD (right)
and his younger brother
HENRI "ROCKET ROCKET" RICHARD (left)

INDEX

PICTURE CREDITS

The publishers would like to thank the following sources for their kind permission to reproduce the pictures in this book.

Alamy: /Gunter Marx: 86–87

Boston Record American Photo by Ray Lussier: 16–17

Courtesy of CCM Hockey: 90–91

Getty Images: 28–29; /Graig Abel/NHLI: 110–111; /Luis Acosta/AFP: 68–69; /Justin K Aller: 70–71; /Claus Andersen: 32–33; /Bruce Bennett: 1, 22–23, 24–25, 64–65, 79, 88–89, 92–93, 95; /Bettmann: 124–125; /Vladimir Bezzubov/KHL Photo Agency: 50–51; /Frederick Breedon: 41; /Fabrice Coffrini/AFP: 30–31; /Jonathan Daniel: 42–43, 118–119; /Andy Devlin/NHLI: 20–21, 108–109; /Melchior DiGiacomo: 10–11; /Focus on Sport: 13; /Gregg Forwerck/NHLI: 82–83; /Leon Halip: 46–47; /Kevin Hoffman: 18–19; /Harry How: 113; /David E Klutho/Sports Illustrated: 120–121; /Robert Laberge: 14–15T, 58–59; /Jim McIsaac: 48–49, 117; /Juan Ocampo/NHLI: 5B, 36–37; /Aaron Ontiveroz/The Denver Post: 72; /Minas Panagiotakis: 30L, 114–115; /Doug Pensinger: 12, 14–15B; /George Pimentel/WireImage: 100–101; /Dave Reginek/NHLI: 38–39; /Vaughn Ridley: 3, 60–61; /Debora Robinson/NHLI: 122–123; /Sean Rudyk/NHLI: 96–97; /John Russell/NHLI: 44–45; /Dave Sandford/NHLI: 5TL, 8–9, 52–53, 62–63, 106–107; /Eliot J Schechter/NHLI: 5TR, 34–35; /Gregory Shamus/NHLI: 26–27; /George Silk/The LIFE Picture Collection: 55; /Don Smith/NHLI: 40, 74–75; /Gerry Thomas/NHLI: 104–105; /Transcendental Graphics: 80–81; /Jeff Vinnick/NHLI: 6–7, 56–57, 84–85, 102–10

PA Images: /Darryl Dyck/The Canadian Press: 98–99

Shutterstock: /REX Features/Mark Stehle/Invasion/AP: 76–77

Cover photographs: all Getty Images. Front: (Mikael Granlund & Brooks Orpik clash) Patrick Smith; (Coyotes & Canucks mascots) Dave Sandford; (Boston Bruins fan) Jim Davis/The Boston Globe; (Scott Wedgewood) Rick Madonna/Toronto Star. Back: (Wayne Gretzky) Bruce Bennett; (Timbits players) Gerry Thomas; (Erie Otters bench) Vaughn Ridley.

Every effort has been made to acknowledge correctly and contact the source and/or copyright holder of each picture, and Carlton Books Limited apologizes for any unintentional errors or omissions that will be corrected in future editions of this book.

ZAMBONI and the configuration of the Zamboni® ice resurfacing machine are registered as trademarks of Frank J. Zamboni & Co., Inc.